FEAST OF FLAVORS
from the Thai Kitchen

FEAST OF **FLAVORS**

from the *Thai* *Kitchen*

A STEP-BY-STEP CULINARY ADVENTURE

Green Frog Publishing

The Publisher wishes to thank **Sia Huat Pte Ltd** for the loan of their crockery and utensils.

National Library of Canada cataloguing in publication
Main entry under title:
Feast of flavors from the Thai kitchen
Includes index.
ISBN 2-89455-171-1
1. Cookery, Thai.
TX724.5.T5F42 2004   641.59593   C2004-940705-8

Project Editor: Jamilah Mohd Hassan
Editor: Lydia Leong
Designer: Geoslyn Lim
Photographer: Sam Yeo
Prop Stylist: Yeo Puay Khoon
Production Co-ordinator: Nor Sidah Haron
Food Preparation: Gourmet Haven

Legal Deposit third quarter 2004
Bibliothèque nationale du Québec and the National Library of Canada
ISBN 2-89455-171-1

Green Frog Publishing is an imprint of Guy Saint-Jean Éditeur Inc.
3154, boul. Industriel, Laval (Québec), Canada H7L 4P7
Tel. (450) 663-1777. Fax. (450) 663-6666.
E-Mail: saint-jean.editeur@qc.aira.com
Web: www.saint-jeanediteur.com

Printed in Singapore

CONTENTS

COOKING TECHNIQUES

Thai cooking is very simple. Its flavors come mainly from the skilful manipulation of certain essential ingredients such Thai basil, chillies, cilantro, coconut cream, garlic, onions, shallots, shrimp paste, lemon grass, fish sauce and soy sauce. In most dishes, very little fat is used and the ingredients are lightly cooked to retain their crunchiness and natural flavor.

The main methods of Thai cooking are stewing, steaming, grilling, baking, stir-frying and deep-frying.

Stewing

Stewing helps to retain all the nutritional goodness and sweetness of the ingredients in the stewing liquid. Tougher cuts of meat can also be used as the cooking process will render them tender. To stew food, the ingredients are usually cut into pieces of similar size and placed into enough liquid to cover them completely. The pot is covered and placed over low heat so the ingredients cook slowly. The stewing liquid is sometimes served as it is to accompany the dish, but it may also be reduced or thickened into gravy.

Steaming

In steaming, the ingredients are cooked by the vapor that rises from the boiling liquid below. As the ingredients do not come in direct contact with the liquid, most of the nutrients are retained, making this a healthy means of cooking food. To get the best results out of steaming food, always use the freshest ingredients.

To steam food, place the ingredients in a flameproof plate or container and place over boiling liquid. Cover tightly with a lid to keep the steam in.

Steaming Glutinous Rice:

In Thailand, glutinous rice is traditionally cooked in a cone-shaped basket set in an urn-shaped pot with a flared mouth (see photograph on left). Rice is washed then soaked for at least 3 hours, but preferably overnight. The basket is lined with muslin and the soaked rice is poured in and covered, first with muslin then with a pot cover. The pot is filled up to a third with water and the basket is positioned to sit in the mouth without touching the water. The water is brought to the boil for about 45 minutes or until translucent and tender.

Without this special basket and pot, glutinous rice can also be steamed using any steamer. If the holes in the steamer basket are large, wrap the soaked rice in muslin or cook it in a flameproof bowl.

Grilling (Broiling)

Grilling is done by setting food above or below a heat source to cook it. This can be done over hot coals/charcoal, under the electric grill, in the oven or even on the top of the stove using a heavy-based pan. In Thai cooking, meats are exposed directly to the heat, or wrapped in leaves and/or aluminum foil. Screwpine (pandan) leaves and banana leaves are commonly used as they impart a lovely fragrance to the cooked food. For successful grilling, the heat must be well-regulated so the food doesn't burn or blacken on the outside too readily while remaining raw on the inside.

Grilling Thai Fish Cakes:

The traditional way of cooking Thai fish cakes is with a flat reddish brown earthenware pan with seven shallow cups or depressions (see photograph on page 8). Each cup is filled with the fish cake paste and covered with small individual dome-shaped caps. The pan is then set to cook over a charcoal fire on an earthenware stove. Once cooked, the entire pan is taken to the table and guests lift the caps to dig out the fish cakes on their own.

An alternative way of cooking fish cakes is by placing the fish cake paste in leaves and grilling or baking. In this book, we have included a recipe for Thai Steamed Fish Mousse (page 67) which is cooked in banana leaf cups and steamed.

Stir-frying

Stir-frying is a quick and fuss-free method of cooking. If you do not have a wok, a large frying pan (skillet) will suffice. Ensure that the wok/pan is hot before adding in the cooking oil. Allow the cooking oil to heat up before adding in your ingredients. Stir them around quickly with a spatula to heat them through. Once the food is cooked, dish out and serve hot.

Because the stir-frying process is so quick, you need to have all the ingredients prepared and on hand before heating up the wok. This will ensure that the ingredients do not overcook or burn as you are busy with the other ingredients.

Note: When stir-frying seafood, toss it quickly to cook. This will seal in the juices without overcooking the seafood. Overcooked seafood will be tough.

Deep-frying

This is a method where food is cooked in a large amount of cooking oil, deep enough to cover it completely. Deep-frying can be done in a wok or in a deep pan. Fill the oil halfway up the wok or pan so that any splattering will be contained. The temperature of the cooking oil is very important when deep-frying. If not hot enough, the food will absorb all the oil and be greasy; but if too hot, the food will burn. The optimum temperature for deep-frying is at 350° F (180° C). Check the temperature with a fat thermometer, or gently lower a morsel of the food for deep-frying in and watch how quickly it browns. If it takes about 45 seconds to a minute, the temperature is right. Continue to monitor the temperature and regulate it by turning the heat down when the oil starts getting hotter.

Have on hand a wire strainer or tongs to remove the deep-fried food from the oil once it is ready. Drain on absorbent paper to remove excess oil. This will also help the food to stay crisp longer.

COOKING UTENSILS

Despite the exotic flavors of Thai food, the cooking utensils are very simple. No special equipment is necessary. This list of basic cooking utensils below will fully equip you for Thai cooking, as well as many other Asian cuisines!

Wok

While you may be able to use a deep pan in place of a wok, having a wok in the kitchen is always a useful tool. The rounded sides of the wok enable food to be easily and continuously moved around over high heat to prevent burning or overcooking when stir-frying. The constant moving of the food around the wok also means that less oil is needed throughout the entire process of stir-frying.

Woks come in various sizes. The size you get should depend on the portion of food you will be cooking each time. Cooking a small amount of food in a large wok will mean that the food will dry up and burn more readily. Cooking a large amount of food in a small wok will also mean that the food will not be in contact with the heat evenly and will take longer to cook. The food will also steam without browning.

When buying your wok, however, do take note of the type of hob you have in the kitchen. Round-bottomed woks work better with gas hobs while flat bottomed woks are more suitable for electric hobs.

Woks with wooden handles will enable you to hold it even when the wok is hot, but those with metal handles mean you have to use oven gloves or a kitchen towel.

Steamer

There are various types of steamers, but the most common are the aluminum multi-tier steamer and the bamboo steamer. The aluminum steamers consist of two or three steamer baskets and a bottom pan. The steamer baskets consist of holes which allow steam from the bottom pan to rise to cook the food. The lid fits the steamer baskets and the bottom pan, so it can be used in any combination.

Bamboo steamers are less expensive than the aluminum type, but sun-dry them after use to prevent mold growth. As they do not come with their own bottom pan, place it snugly in a wok or pan of boiling water. Should a steamer not be available, place the ingredients on a heatproof plate and stand it on a rack or overturned flameproof bowl over boiling water in a large wok or pan. Cover tightly, preferably with a domed pot cover, to steam.

Cleaver

A cleaver is useful for separating bones from meat, tenderizing meat, finely shredding vegetables and also smashing garlic. This multi-use kitchen tool is rather heavy, but the weight is inversely proportional to the amount of effort required to use it. That is, the heavier the cleaver, the less effort required in using it. Thus, when buying a cleaver, choose the heaviest one that you are comfortable with.

Spatula

There are various kinds of spatulas, but in Thai cooking, a wooden spatula is useful for stir frying. The rounded corners of the spatula enable food to be easily moved around in the wok without scratching the non-stick surface. As a non-conductor of heat, the wooden spatula will also not heat up in the process of cooking.

Wire Strainer

A wire strainer is useful for removing deep-fried foods from fat quickly. It allows the oil to drain away while keeping the food crisp. In Thai cooking, a wire strainer is also useful for removing noodles quickly after blanching them in hot water. The slippery noodles are held in the strainer while the water drains away.

Mortar and Pestle

A mortar and pestle is useful for grinding and pounding small amounts of seeds, herbs and spices. It allows you to control the process, so you can obtain a coarse or fine paste as preferred. This is not always achievable with an electric blender. A mortar and pestle also releases the oils and fragrance of herbs and spices more effectively. The resulting mixture or paste can then be easily scraped from the mortar with a spoon with minimal wastage.

WEIGHTS & MEASURES

Quantities for this book are given in Metric and American (spoon and cup) measures. Standard spoon and cup measurements used are: 1 teaspoon = 5 ml, 1 dessertspoon = 10 ml, 1 tablespoon = 15 ml, 1 cup = 250 ml. All measures are level unless otherwise stated.

DRY MEASURES

Metric	Imperial
30 grams	1 ounce
45 grams	1^1/$_2$ ounces
55 grams	2 ounces
70 grams	2^1/$_2$ ounces
85 grams	3 ounces
100 grams	3^1/$_2$ ounces
110 grams	4 ounces
125 grams	4^1/$_2$ ounces
140 grams	5 ounces
280 grams	10 ounces
450 grams	16 ounces (1 pound)
500 grams	1 pound, 1^1/$_2$ ounces
700 grams	1^1/$_2$ pounds
800 grams	1^3/$_4$ pounds
1 kilogram	2 pounds, 3 ounces
1.5 kilograms	3 pounds, 4^1/$_2$ ounces
2 kilograms	4 pounds, 6 ounces

LENGTH

Metric	Imperial
0.5 cm	^{1}/$_4$ inch
1 cm	^{1}/$_2$ inch
1.5 cm	^{3}/$_4$ inch
2.5 cm	1 inch

LIQUID AND VOLUME MEASURES

Metric	Imperial	American
5 ml	^{1}/$_6$ fl oz	1 teaspoon
10 ml	^{1}/$_3$ fl oz	1 dessertspoon
15 ml	^{1}/$_2$ fl oz	1 tablespoon
60 ml	2 fl oz	^{1}/$_4$ cup (4 tablespoons)
85 ml	2^1/$_2$ fl oz	^{1}/$_3$ cup
90 ml	3 fl oz	^{3}/$_8$ cup (6 tablespoons)
125 ml	4 fl oz	^{1}/$_2$ cup
180 ml	6 fl oz	^{3}/$_4$ cup
250 ml	8 fl oz	1 cup
300 ml	10 fl oz (^{1}/$_2$ pint)	1^1/$_4$ cups
375 ml	12 fl oz	1^1/$_2$ cups
435 ml	14 fl oz	1^3/$_4$ cups
500 ml	16 fl oz	2 cups
625 ml	20 fl oz (1 pint)	2^1/$_2$ cups
750 ml	24 fl oz (1^1/$_5$ pints)	3 cups
1 liter	32 fl oz (1^3/$_5$ pints)	4 cups
1.25 liters	40 fl oz (2 pints)	5 cups
1.5 liters	48 fl oz (2^2/$_5$ pints)	6 cups
2.5 liters	80 fl oz (4 pints)	10 cups

OVEN TEMPERATURE

Regulo	°C	°F	Gas
Very slow	120	250	1
Slow	150	300	2
Moderately slow	160	325	3
Moderate	180	350	4
Moderately hot	190/200	370/400	5/6
Hot	210/220	410/440	6/7
Very hot	230	450	8
Super hot	250/290	475/550	9/10

ABBREVIATION

Tbsp	tablespoon
tsp	teaspoon
kg	kilogram
g	gram
l	liters
ml	milliliters
oz	ounce
lb	pound
in	inch

SOUPS

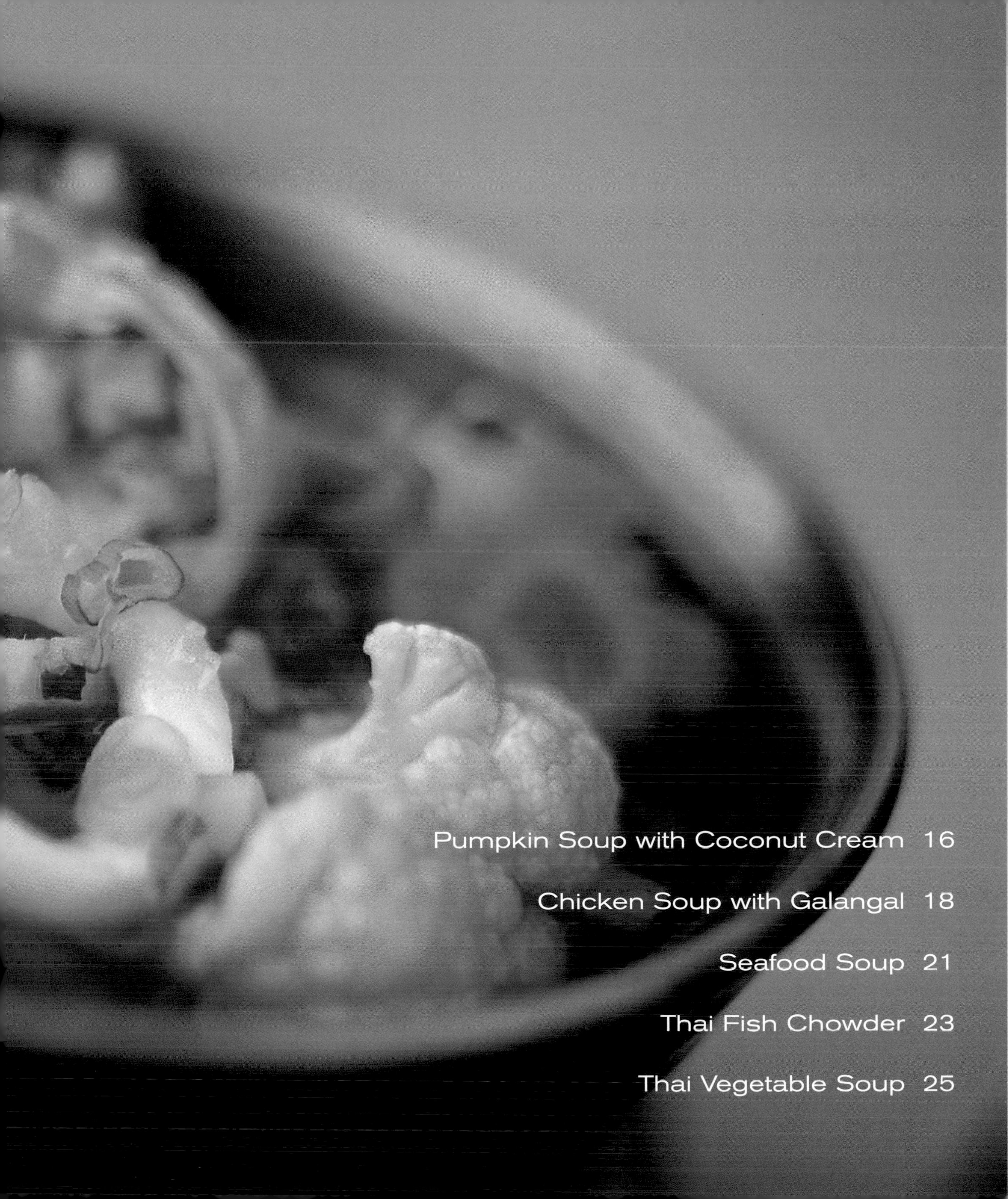

Cut the pumpkin flesh into bite-sized pieces.

Pound the ingredients with a mortar and pestle to regulate the consistency of the paste.

Put the paste gently into the coconut cream and stir to mix well.

PUMPKIN SOUP WITH COCONUT CREAM

A coconut milk-based soup laced with prawns and pumpkin pieces.

Ingredients

Pumpkin	³/₄ lb (350 g)
Lemon juice	1 Tbsp
Shrimps	¹/₄ lb (125 g), shelled
Shallots	2, peeled and chopped
Dried shrimp paste *(kapi)*	1 Tbsp (15 g)
Bird's eye chillies	2
Water	1 cup (250 ml)
Coconut cream	3 cups (750 ml)
Ground white pepper	to taste
Thai sweet basil *(bai horapa)* leaves	a handful

Method

- Slice pumpkin in half and scoop out seeds. Skin and cut flesh into rectangular pieces. Sprinkle pumpkin flesh with lemon juice. Set aside.
- Pound shrimps with shallots, shrimp paste and chillies, adding a little of the water if necessary, to form a well-mixed paste.

- Pour half the coconut cream into a pan. Add shrimp mixture and bring to the boil. Reduce heat and stir with a wooden spoon to ensure a smooth consistency.
- Add pumpkin flesh and cook gently for 10 minutes. Pour in remaining coconut cream and water. Season with pepper.

- Cover pan and leave to simmer for a further 10 minutes until pumpkin flesh is tender but not mushy. Stir in basil leaves and serve immediately.

Remove the tough outer layers of the lemon grass and discard. Slice with a sharp cleaver.

Add the chicken a few pieces at a time to avoid them from sticking together when cooked.

The kaffir lime leaves will add a refreshing citrus flavor to the soup.

S
T
E
P
-
B
Y
-
S
T
E
P

CHICKEN SOUP WITH GALANGAL

A wholesome chicken soup with the unique peppery flavor of galangal and the refreshing taste of lemon grass and kaffir lime leaves.

Ingredients

Water	1 cup (250 ml)
Coconut milk	4 cups (1 liter)
Chicken thighs	8, sliced or 1¼ lb (600 g) chicken breast, diced
Lemon grass	2 stalks, cut into 1 in (2.5 cm) lengths
Galangal	½ in (1 cm) knob, peeled and finely sliced
Fish sauce (nam pla)	2 Tbsp
Bird's eye chillies	3
Kaffir lime leaves	3
Lemon juice	2 Tbsp

Garnish

Red chilli	1, shredded
Scallion	1, chopped

Method

- Bring water to the boil with half the coconut milk.
- Add chicken, lemon grass, galangal and 1 Tbsp fish sauce. Simmer for about 20 minutes or until chicken is cooked. Less cooking time will be required for diced chicken breast.
- Stir in remaining coconut milk and turn up heat. As soon as it begins to boil, toss in whole chillies and kaffir lime leaves. Stir and remove from heat.
- Serve in individual bowls. Sprinkle with lemon juice and fish sauce to taste. Garnish with chilli and scallion.

SEAFOOD SOUP

A clear soup with long beans, cauliflower, turnip, carrot, pickled mustard, catfish, shrimp and squid.

Ingredients

Tamarind pulp	5 oz (140 g)
Water	6 cups (1.5 liters)
Catfish	1, about 10 oz (280 g), deboned and sliced into 2 in (5 cm) pieces
Long beans	¼ lb (110 g), cut into 1 in (2.5 cm) lengths
Cauliflower florets	¼ lb (110 g)
Turnip	¼ lb (110 g), peeled and cut into ¼ in (0.5 cm) thick slices
Carrot	2 oz (55 g), peeled and cut into ¼ in (0.5 cm) thick slices
Pickled mustard	¼ lb (110 g), cut into ¾ in (1.5 cm) pieces
Palm sugar (jaggery)	2 Tbsp, crushed or brown sugar
Fish sauce (nam pla)	⅓ cup (90 ml)
Shrimps	10 oz (280 g), shelled and deveined
Squid	¼ lb (110 g), cleaned and cut into rings

Paste

Dried chillies	8, seeded, soaked in hot water and drained
Shallots	6, peeled
Dried shrimp paste (kapi)	1 in (2.5 cm) square
Garlic	5 cloves, peeled

Garnish

Scallion	1, finely chopped

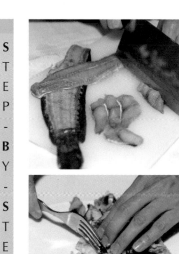

Debone the catfish by slicing down the length of the fish with a sharp knife. Slice the fillets.

Shred the cooked fish with a fork. Discard the skin.

While the soup is boiling, add the rest of the ingredients and continue to boil until the vegetables are tender.

Method

- Combine tamarind pulp and ⅓ cup (90 ml) water. Strain and extract juice. Set aside.
- Combine paste ingredients and blend (process) until fine.
- Boil remaining water, add finely ground paste and catfish and continue to boil for 5–10 minutes.

- Remove catfish and set aside to cool. Shred fish and return to soup.
- Add long beans, cauliflower, turnip, carrot, pickled mustard, palm sugar or brown sugar, fish sauce, shrimps, squid and tamarind juice. Boil for 5–8 minutes. Serve, garnished with scallion.

THAI FISH CHOWDER

A hot and spicy fish soup with a distinct lemony flavor of lemon grass and kaffir lime leaves.

Ingredients

Cooking oil	2 Tbsp
Dried chillies	15
Garlic	6 cloves, peeled
Shallots	8, peeled
Chicken stock	4 cups (1 liter) (see page 31)
Cilantro roots	3, bruised
Lemon grass	3 stalks, bruised and halved
Kaffir lime leaves	5
Galangal	2 in (5 cm) knob, peeled and finely sliced
Fish sauce *(nam pla)*	¼ cup (60 ml)
Bird's eye chillies	8, bruised
Salt	1 tsp
Spanish mackerel fillet	1 lb (500 g), cut into 1 in (2.5 cm) pieces

Garnish

Cilantro	1 sprig, cut into ½ in (1 cm) lengths

STEP-BY-STEP

Frying the dried chillies will enhance their fragrance and the flavor of the dish it is used in.

Stir the soup to ensure the ingredients are well-mixed.

Add the mackerel pieces into the soup one by one so they do not stick to one another.

Method

- Heat cooking oil and stir-fry dried chillies until crisp. Remove and drain well.
- In the same oil, fry garlic and shallots for about 2–3 minutes or until light brown. Remove and drain well.
- Combine fried dried chillies, garlic and shallots and grind together into a fine paste.
- Bring chicken stock to the boil. Add coriander roots, lemon grass, kaffir lime leaves, galangal, fish sauce, bird's eye chillies and salt. Stir well and continue to boil for about 5 minutes.
- Add ground paste and mackerel and cook for another 5 minutes. Spoon into bowls and garnish with cilantro leaves.

THAI VEGETABLE SOUP

A spicy vegetable soup filled with the wholesome goodness of carrot, sponge gourd, oyster mushrooms and baby corn cobs.

Ingredients

Chicken stock or water	5 cups (1.25 liters) (see page 31)
Lemon grass	1 stalk, bruised
Fish sauce *(nam pla)*	1/4 cup (60 ml)
Carrot	1, peeled and cut into 1 1/2 in (3.5 cm) lengths
Bird's eye chillies	4
Sponge (bottle) gourd	1 lb (500 g), peeled and cut into 1 1/2 in (3.5 cm) strips
Fresh oyster mushrooms	5 oz (150 g)
Baby corn cobs	8, cut into 1 1/2 in (3.5 cm) lengths
Thai sweet basil *(bai horapa)*	2 sprigs, plucked
Salt	to taste

Paste

White peppercorns	10
Dried shrimp paste *(kapi)*	1 in (2.5 cm) square
Fish sauce *(nam pla)*	3 Tbsp
Shallots	10, peeled
Dried shrimps	5 oz (150 g), soaked and drained

Garnish

Crisp-fried shallots	1 Tbsp
Bird's eye chillies	3–4
Red chilli	1, chopped

Slice the carrot into 1 1/2 in (3.5 cm) lengths then slice in half and cut into smaller pieces.

Cutting the vegetables into pieces of similar size will help them cook more evenly together, while being visually pleasing.

Thai sweet basil adds a lovely but strong anise flavor to dishes. Do not add more than is specified in recipes.

Method

- Combine paste ingredients and grind until fine.
- Bring chicken stock or water to the boil, add finely ground paste and lemon grass. Simmer for 15 minutes.
- Add fish sauce, carrot and bird's eye chillies and boil for 3 minutes.
- Add sponge gourd, mushrooms and baby corn. Boil for another 5 minutes.
- Stir in basil leaves and season with salt.
- Serve hot, garnished with crisp-fried shallots, bird's eye chillies and chopped red chillies.

Cut the red bell pepper into strips using a cleaver or sharp knife.

Stir the shrimp paste quickly with a spoon to dilute.

Use a wok ladle to break up the lumps of rice while pouring into the wok.

FRIED RICE WITH SHRIMP PASTE

A simple rice dish made fragrant with shrimp paste.

Ingredients

Shrimp paste	2 Tbsp
Water	2 Tbsp
Cooked rice	$1^3/_4$ lb (750 g)
Cooking oil	3 Tbsp
Garlic	2 cloves, peeled and crushed
Salt	to taste
Dried shrimps	2 Tbsp, finely ground

Garnish

Shallots	4, peeled and finely sliced
Red bell pepper	$^1/_4$, cut into strips
Omelette	cooked using 2 eggs, thinly sliced
Lemon	1, cut into quarters

Method

- Dilute shrimp paste in water and mix well with cooked rice.
- Heat oil and brown garlic. Add rice and sauté over medium heat for 5 minutes, adding salt to taste. Sprinkle finely ground dried shrimps over rice. Remove from heat.
- Serve garnished with shallots, red bell pepper, slices of omelette and lemon quarters.

28

Crush the garlic and bird's eye chillies using the flat of a cleaver.

Brown garlic and chilli in hot oil to bring out the fragrance.

Sprinkle in fish sauce and stir-fry to mix.

S T E P - B Y - S T E P

FRIED RICE WITH CHICKEN AND BASIL

A quick and tasty dish made using some of Thailand's favorite ingredients—fish sauce and Thai sweet basil.

Ingredients

Cooking oil	$1/4$ cup (60 ml)
Garlic	2 cloves, peeled and crushed
Bird's eye chillies (red)	2, crushed
Chicken breast	10 oz (300 g), finely sliced
Fish sauce *(nam pla)*	2 Tbsp
Thai sweet basil *(bai horapa)*	20 leaves
Cooked rice	$1^3/4$ lb (750 g)

Garnish

Shallot	1, peeled, finely sliced and crisp-fried

Method

- Heat oil and lightly brown garlic and chilli. Add chicken and sauté for 2–3 minutes before mixing in fish sauce and basil leaves.
- Take out a few basil leaves and reserve for garnish then add rice. Sauté over strong heat for 3 minutes, stirring briskly. Remove from heat.
- Transfer to a large serving dish or individual bowls. Garnish with reserved basil leaves and fried shallot.
- Serve with fish sauce with chopped bird's eye chillies.

PORK FRIED RICE WITH TOMATO SAUCE

A unique combination of rice stir-fried with meat and tomato sauce.

Ingredients

Cooking oil	2 Tbsp
Garlic	3 cloves, crushed
Pork or chicken	10 oz (300 g), finely sliced
Onion	1, peeled and diced
Fish sauce (nam pla)	2 Tbsp
Canned tomato purée	3 Tbsp
Cooked rice	1³/₄ lb (750 g)
Ground white pepper	to taste

Garnish

Cucumber	1, sliced into rounds
Scallions	4
Cilantro leaves (optional)	1 sprig
Lemon (optional)	1

STEP-BY-STEP

Use a cleaver to slice the cucumber for even rounds.

Check the liquid content after adding the tomato purée. Add a little water and oil if it is too dry.

Use a wok ladle to mix the ingredients and rice thoroughly.

Method

- Heat oil and brown garlic. Add pork or chicken and sauté for about 3 minutes.
- Add onion, fish sauce and tomato purée. Stir well, adding a little water and oil if the mixture becomes too dry.
- Turn up heat. When mixture is cooked after about 3 minutes more, add rice and sauté for a further 3 minutes. Season to taste with pepper.

- Serve in a large dish, garnished with cucumber rounds and spring onions. If desired, sprinkle with cilantro leaves. Squeeze lemon juice over the rice if you like it sour.

PINEAPPLE RICE

A dish of stir-fried rice sweetened with pineapple cubes and made complete with chicken and chicken sausage.

Ingredients

Thai fragrant rice	1¹/₂ cup (375 ml), washed and drained
Water	2¹/₂ cups (625 ml)
Ripe pineapple	1, about 3 lb (1.5 kg)
Cooking oil	3 Tbsp
Shallots	10, peeled and sliced
Dried shrimps	3 oz (85 g), soaked in hot water for 5 minutes, drained and chopped
Chicken breast	10 oz (280 g), cut into small cubes
Chicken sausages	4, cut into small cubes
Fish sauce (nam pla)	3 Tbsp
Meat curry powder (optional)	2 Tbsp
Light soy sauce	¹/₄ cup (60 ml)
Sugar	1¹/₂ Tbsp

Garnish

Lettuce leaves	
Cilantro leaves	2 oz (55 g), chopped
Red chilli	1, cut into small strips and soaked in cold water

S T E P - B Y - S T E P

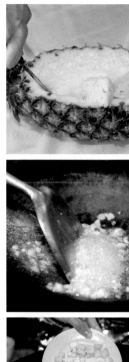

Use a small sharp knife to cut around the edge of the pineapple to extract the flesh.

Cook the chicken cubes in hot oil to seal in the juices while retaining the tenderness.

Add the pineapple cubes at the final stage so as not to overcook them.

Method

- Combine rice and water and cook. Fluff rice and set aside to cool.
- Cut pineapple in half lengthways. Run a knife around the edge of pineapple, cut and scoop out flesh. Cut flesh into ¹/₂ in (1 cm) cubes to get 1 cup (250 ml). Keep shell (casing) aside.
- Heat cooking oil and fry shallots until brown and crisp. Set aside. In the same oil sauté dried shrimps until fragrant. Add chicken and sausage cubes and fry until chicken is cooked.
- Add fish sauce, meat curry powder (optional), soy sauce, sugar and cooked rice. Mix well. Add pineapple cubes and fry for 2–3 minutes. Set aside.
- Heat pineapple shell (casing) in a 350°F (180°C) preheated oven for 10 minutes. Remove from oven and fill with pineapple fried rice.
- Garnish rice with lettuce, crisp-fried shallots, cilantro leaves and chilli strips.

SPICY FRIED NOODLES WITH SEAFOOD

A light, tasty dish of flat rice noodles stir-fried with fresh seafood.

Ingredients

Seafood (squid, shelled shrimp, fish meat, steamed mussels)	1 lb (500 g)
Cooking oil	5 oz (150 ml)
Garlic	3 Tbsp, peeled and crushed
Light soy sauce	2 Tbsp
Thick flat rice noodles (sen yai)	1 lb (500 g)
Fish sauce (nam pla)	3 Tbsp
Holy basil (bai gkaprow) leaves	a handful, crisp-fried
Red chillies	3, roughly chopped
Ground white pepper	to taste

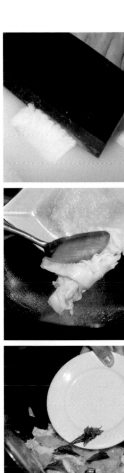

Slit the squid tubes and lay them flat. Score them so they curl up nicely when cooked.

Break the thick rice noodles up as you add it to the wok.

Adding fried basil leaves gives the dish a unique Thai flavor.

Method

- Cut seafood into pieces if necessary.
- Heat ¼ cup (60 ml) oil and brown garlic. Sauté seafood for a few minutes in the same oil. Drain and set aside.
- Add remaining oil to the wok and increase heat. Add soy sauce and noodles and sauté for 2–3 minutes. Add cooked seafood and fish sauce. Stir well.
- Add basil leaves and chillies and stir. Add pepper to taste and cook for a minute more.
- Serve hot, garnished with red chilli strips if desired.

Prepare the thickener in advance so you have it on hand when required.

Drain the noodles well before adding to the wok to prevent the final dish from becoming too soggy.

Sauté the noodles briskly to dry and heat them through.

NOODLES WITH MEAT SAUCE

Thin egg noodles served with minced meat and a light sauce.

Ingredients

Dried egg noodles	1 lb (500 g)
Lettuce leaves	6
Cooking oil	5 oz (150 ml)
Garlic	1 tsp, peeled and chopped
Dark soy sauce	$1/2$ Tbsp
Shallot	2 Tbsp, peeled and chopped
Beef	14 oz (400 g), minced or ground
Water	$1/2$ cup (125 ml)
Curry powder	$1/4$ cup (60 ml)
Light soy sauce	3 Tbsp
All-purpose flour	$1/2$ tsp, blended with 2 Tbsp water
Salt	to taste
Ground white pepper	to taste

Garnish

Cilantro leaves	1 sprig, chopped

Method

- Cook noodles in boiling water according to the instructions on the packet. Drain.
- Line a salad bowl with lettuce leaves and set aside.
- Heat $1/3$ cup (90 ml) oil and brown garlic. Add noodles and sauté for 1–2 minutes, adding dark soy sauce. Place noodles in prepared salad bowl.

- Heat remaining oil and brown shallot. Add meat, water, curry powder and light soy sauce. Stir well. When sauce begins to boil, stir in blended flour and add salt and pepper to taste.
- Simmer for a few minutes, before pouring mixture over noodles. Garnish with cilantro leaves to serve.

Slice the omelettes thinly using a sharp cleaver in an up and down motion.

Cooking the shallots in coconut cream adds a unique flavor to this dish.

Use a wok ladle to mix the ingredients thoroughly.

STEP-BY-STEP

RICE VERMICELLI IN COCONUT MILK

Rice vermicelli, lightly flavored with coconut milk, served with generous helpings of chicken, shrimps and bean sprouts.

Ingredients

Tamarind pulp	2 oz (55 g)
Water	2 Tbsp
Boiled coconut cream (see recipe p.41)	1 cup (250 ml)
Shallots	6, peeled and chopped
Chicken fillet	3 oz (100 g), thinly sliced
Tiger shrimps	5 oz (150 g), medium-sized, shelled and deveined
Preserved soy bean paste (tau jiew)	2 Tbsp
Sugar	2 Tbsp
Chilli powder	2 Tbsp
Rice vermicelli	$^1/_2$ lb (250 g), soaked for 15 minutes or until soft, drained
Fried bean curd	1, finely diced
Chinese chives	$^1/_4$ lb (100 g), cut into 1 in (2.5 cm) lengths
Cilantro leaves	2 oz (50 g), cut into 1 in (2.5 cm) lengths
Eggs	2, beaten, fried into thin omelettes and cut into strips
Bean sprouts	10 oz (300 g), tailed
Lemons	2, cut in wedges
Banana blossom (dok kluai)	1, tough outer layers discarded, shredded then blanched and drained

Method

- Combine tamarind pulp and water and extract juice. Set aside.
- Heat boiled coconut cream for 5 minutes, then add shallots and stir-fry until fragrant.
- Add chicken and shrimps and continue stir-frying for 2 minutes.

- Add preserved soy bean paste, sugar, chilli powder and tamarind juice and mix well into a sauce. Divide sauce into two portions and keep one portion aside.
- Add rice vermicelli, bean curd and Chinese chives to one portion of the sauce and cook for 1 minute.

- Transfer to a serving dish and pour reserved sauce on top of vermicelli.
- Garnish with cilantro leaves and omelette strips.
- Serve with bean sprouts, lemon wedges and blanched banana blossom.

BOILED COCONUT CREAM

Ingredients
Water	1³/₄ cup (435 ml)
Grated coconut	1 lb (500 g)

Method
- Combine water and grated coconut. Squeeze to obtain coconut milk.
- Boil coconut milk until it separates and milk is reduced to 1 cup (250 ml).

Slice the beef as thin as possible so it cooks quickly and will not be too tough.

Watch the stock as it boils so that it does not boil over.

Cook the beef slices briskly or to the level of doneness that you prefer.

BEEF NOODLE SOUP

Thai comfort food—thin rice noodles served in a bowl of warm beef stock with slices of beef.

Ingredients

Beef stock (see recipe p.43)	5 cups (1.25 liters)
Garlic	2 cloves + 1 Tbsp, peeled and chopped
Celery	2 stalks
Fish sauce *(nam pla)*	2 Tbsp
Light soy sauce	2 Tbsp
Ground white pepper	to taste
Beef fillet	10 oz (300 g), cut into thin strips
Thin rice noodles	1 lb (500 g)
Cooking oil	2 Tbsp
Cilantro leaves	½ Tbsp, chopped
Scallion	½ Tbsp, chopped
Chilli powder	to taste
Lemon juice or vinegar	2 Tbsp

Method

- Heat stock with whole garlic cloves, celery, fish sauce, soy sauce and pepper. Cover and simmer for 10 minutes. Remove garlic and celery. Bring stock to a full boil.
- Place beef fillet in a straining spoon or strainer and hold in the boiling stock for 30 seconds. Remove and drain. Reduce heat.
- Cook noodles in the simmering stock for 2 minutes, then remove and drain. Meanwhile heat oil and lightly brown chopped garlic.
- Serve soup in individual bowls. First place noodles in each bowl and sprinkle with cilantro, scallion, browned garlic, chilli powder and pepper. Add meat, a few drops of lemon juice or vinegar and pour stock over.

STOCK

This is a classic soup base which can be prepared in advance and frozen until needed. Use either chicken, pork or beef bones as required. When a vegetable stock is required, omit the meat bones.

Ingredients

Water	8 cups (2 liters)
Meat bones (optional)	2 lb (1 kg)
Garlic	2 cloves
Turnip	1, medium
Celery	2 stalks
Shallots	2
Ground ginger	a pinch
Ground black pepper	to taste

Method

- Bring all the ingredients to the boil in a large pot over medium heat.
- Lower heat and simmer for 1 hour. Strain and use as required.

Pull the duck meat away from the bone with one hand and use a knife to cut away the bone with the other hand.

Put the duck meat carefully into the curry to avoid splattering.

Add in the peas, tomatoes and chillies and stir them into the curry to cook them.

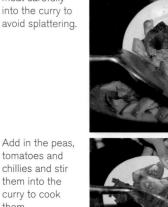

S
T
E
P
-
B
Y
-
S
T
E
P

DUCK WITH CURRY

A unique dish of roast duck in a spicy red curry. This dish goes well with plain white rice.

Ingredients

Roast duck	1, medium-sized
Coconut cream	3 cups (750 ml)
Water	½ cup (125 ml)
Red curry paste (see recipe p.47)	2–3 Tbsp
Kaffir lime leaves	10
Fish sauce (nam pla)	3 Tbsp
Frozen peas	3 oz (75 g)
Tomatoes	5, small, cut in half
Red or green chillies	4, cut into strips
Thai sweet basil (bai horapa)	1 sprig

Method

- Debone duck and cut into bite-sized pieces.
- Bring half the coconut cream to the boil with water. Leave to simmer.
- In a wok, bring to the boil a third of the remaining coconut cream, then stir in red curry paste. Cook for a few minutes before adding bergamot leaves and pieces of duck. Stir well.
- Add simmering coconut cream and turn up the heat.
- Add fish sauce, peas, tomatoes and chillies. Simmer until peas are cooked then add remaining coconut cream and bring to the boil.
- Sprinkle with basil leaves and remove from heat. Serve with plain rice.

RED CURRY PASTE

Ingredients

Cumin seeds	2 tsp
Coriander seeds	1 tsp
Dried chillies	8, soaked, drained and coarsely chopped
Kaffir lime rind	$^{1}/_{2}$ tsp, finely chopped
Salt	1 tsp
Lemon grass	1 tsp, finely chopped
Garlic	1 Tbsp, peeled and chopped
Galangal	1 Tbsp, peeled and chopped
Shrimp paste *(kapi)*	1 Tbsp

Method

- Place cumin and coriander seeds in a pan without adding any oil. Dry-fry over medium heat for 1–2 minutes until they are slightly browned and aromatic.
- Combine all the ingredients and pound into a paste. Keep in an airtight jar in the refrigerator and use as needed.

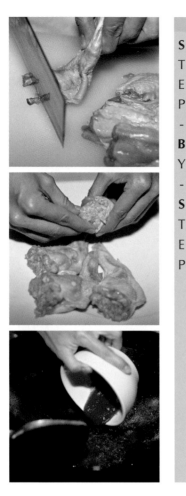

Using a cleaver, carefully scrape the chicken meat away from the bones.

Pack the chicken wings tightly with stuffing so that the filling does not shrink and fall out when cooking.

Pour in the chilli sauce, tomato sauce and sugar into the remaining oil and mix well.

STUFFED CHICKEN WINGS

A dish of fried chicken wings taken a step further by removing the bones and stuffing with additional minced meat.

Ingredients

Chicken wings	8–12
Cilantro roots	5, chopped
White peppercorns	10
Garlic	3 cloves, peeled
Pork	14 oz (400 g), minced (ground)
Light soy sauce	2 Tbsp
Cooking oil	1 cup (250 ml)
Cilantro leaves	a handful

Sauce

Chilli sauce	2 Tbsp
Tomato sauce	3 Tbsp
Sugar	1 Tbsp

Garnish

Lettuce leaves	5
Tomatoes	2

Method

- Debone chicken wings leaving the tips intact. Be careful not to tear the skin.
- Pound together cilantro roots, peppercorns and garlic. Mix in pork and sprinkle with a little soy sauce.

- Stuff chicken wings with pork mixture. Heat oil over medium heat and fry stuffed chicken wings until golden. Sprinkle in coriander leaves while frying. Remove cooked chicken wings and drain.

- To make the sauce, pour chilli sauce, tomato sauce, sugar and remaining soy sauce into oil used for frying. Bring to the boil and simmer for 2 minutes.
- Serve chicken wings with the sauce on the side.

THAI CHICKEN CURRY

A spicy chicken curry that goes well with white rice. For a less spicy dish, remove the seeds from the dried chillies before using.

Ingredients

Paste

Shallots	10, peeled
Garlic	4 cloves, peeled
Lemon grass	4 stalks
Cilantro roots	6
Galangal	½ in (1 cm) knob, peeled
Coriander seeds	1 Tbsp
Ground black pepper	2 tsp
Kaffir lime rind	grated from 1 kaffir lime
Kaffir lime leaves	2
Dried chillies	15–20, seeded if preferred
Shrimp paste *(kapi)*	2 tsp, crushed
Cooking oil	¼ cup (60 ml)
Chicken	2 lb (1 kg), cut into 8–10 pieces
Coconut milk	4 cups (1 liter)
Pickled bamboo shoots	½ lb (200 g)
Kaffir lime leaves	3
Fish sauce *(nam pla)*	2 Tbsp
Salt	to taste
Sugar	to taste
Thai sweet basil *(bai horapa)*	2 oz (50 g), chopped

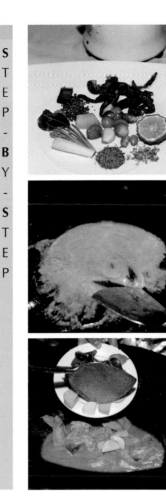

STEP-BY-STEP

Prepare all the ingredients for the paste and blend using an electric blender.

Stir the curry around a little even as it is simmering to prevent it from burning.

Lower the ingredients in carefully to avoid the curry splattering.

Method

- Blend (process) paste ingredients until fine.
- Heat cooking oil and sauté finely ground paste until fragrant. Stir in chicken and coconut milk. Simmer over low heat for 20 minutes.

- When chicken is tender, add bamboo shoots, kaffir lime leaves, fish sauce, salt, sugar and basil leaves. Cook for another 10 minutes, remove from heat and serve.

FRIED CHICKEN IN SCREWPINE LEAF

The screwpine leaves give additional fragrance and add a unique touch to this delightful dish.

Ingredients

Chicken fillet	1 lb (500 g), cut into small pieces
Sugar	1 Tbsp
Sesame oil	1 Tbsp
Fish sauce (nam pla)	2 Tbsp
Dark soy sauce	1 tsp
Screwpine leaves (bai toey)	15
Cooking oil for deep-frying	2 cups (500 ml)

Paste

Garlic	4 cloves, peeled
Ground white pepper	1 tsp
Cilantro	3 sprigs, chopped
Shallots	4, peeled
Lemon grass	1 stalk, thinly sliced
Preserved soy beans	1 Tbsp

S T E P - B Y - S T E P

Chopping the cilantro releases the full flavor of the herb.

Mix the finely ground paste well into the chicken pieces so the flavor goes well into the meat.

Fold a screwpine leaf to create a cone. Place the chicken inside and tuck the ends of the leaf in through the cone to create a tight parcel. Trim off excess leaf.

Method

- Combine paste ingredients and blend until fine.
- Mix chicken with finely ground paste. Add sugar, sesame oil, fish sauce, dark soy sauce and marinate for 30 minutes.
- Wrap marinated chicken in screwpine leaves.
- Deep-fry wrapped chicken for 10–12 minutes or until screwpine leaves turn a dark green.
- Remove from oil and drain. Allow guests to unwrap the chicken on their own.

Leave the boiled chicken to cool before slicing or it will be too hot to handle.

Slice the cucumber finely so that it complements the subtle flavors of the dish.

Mix the dressing into the salad bit by bit to ensure that it is well mixed.

SPICY CHICKEN SALAD

A light and refreshing salad that can be served as part of a main meal or as an appetizer.

Ingredients

Bird's eye chillies	10, coarsely pounded
Roasted chilli paste (nam prik pau) (see recipe p. 55)	2 Tbsp
Fish sauce (nam pla)	2 Tbsp
Palm sugar (jaggery)	1 Tbsp, crushed or brown sugar
Lemon or lime juice	3 Tbsp
Coconut milk	¼ cup (60 ml)
Chicken breast	½ lb (250 g), boiled for 10 minutes or until tender, then sliced
Lemon grass	6 stalks, finely sliced
Kaffir lime leaves	4, finely sliced
Cilantro leaves	2 oz (50 g), finely sliced
Mint leaves	3 oz (100 g), finely sliced + extra for garnishing

Garnish

Lettuce leaves	10
Tomatoes	2, cut into wedges
Red chillies	3, seeded and cut into strips
Cucumber	1, cut in half and finely sliced
Radish	1, peeled and sliced

Method

- Blend (process) bird's eye chillies, roasted chilli paste, fish sauce, palm or brown sugar, lemon or lime juice and coconut milk into a salty-sour dressing.
- Mix chicken with lemon grass, kaffir lime leaves, cilantro leaves and mint.
- Add dressing and mix well. Serve on a dish lined with lettuce leaves.
- Garnish with tomatoes, red chilli strips, mint leaves, cucumber and radish.

ROASTED CHILLI PASTE

Ingredients

Cooking oil	3 cups (750 ml)
Shallots	10 oz (280 g), peeled and sliced
Garlic	10 oz (280 g), peeled and sliced
Dried shrimps	10 oz (280 g), soaked and drained
Dried shrimp paste *(kapi)*	1 in (2.5 cm) piece, roasted and crushed
Dried chillies	1/3 lb (170 g), seeded, soaked and drained
Palm sugar (jaggery)	3/4 cup (180 ml), crushed or brown sugar
Fish sauce *(nam pla)*	1/4 cup (60 ml)
Tamarind juice	1/4 cup (60 ml), from 2 Tbsp tamarind pulp and 1/4 cup (60 ml) water
Salt	2 tsp

Method

- Heat oil and fry shallots and garlic until golden brown. Remove and drain.
- In the same oil, fry dried shrimp, shrimp paste and chillies for 3 minutes until golden brown. Cool the oil.
- Combine fried ingredients and palm or brown sugar and pound into a fine paste.
- Add fish sauce, tamarind juice, salt and cooled oil. Blend to get a fine paste. Store in an airtight jar and use as needed.

BEEF CUTLETS IN EGG NETS

An attractive and colorful dish that is commonly served as an appetizer.
Replace the beef with chicken or pork as desired.

Ingredients

Beef	³/₄ lb (350 g), minced (ground)
Shrimps	3 oz (100 g), shelled and minced (ground)
Cooking oil	¹/₃ cup (90 ml)
Onion	1, large, peeled and finely diced
Garlic	1 Tbsp, peeled and minced (ground)
Roasted groundnuts	2 oz (70 g), ground
Cilantro roots	1 Tbsp, chopped
Ground white pepper	1 tsp
Fish sauce (nam pla)	3 Tbsp
Sugar	1 Tbsp
Eggs	6, beaten
Cilantro leaves	1 sprig, stalk removed
Red chilli	1, seeded and cut into thin strips

Garnish

Cucumber	1, peeled and sliced
Scallion	1, chopped
Carrot	1, peeled and chopped

S T E P - B Y - S T E P

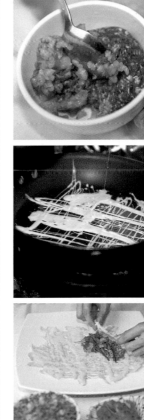

Fold the minced shrimps into the minced beef to mix well.

Allow the egg to cook slowly over low heat so that it remains soft and can be folded easily without breaking.

To assemble, place the filling close to the edge of the egg net. Fold the edge over and roll once. Fold the sides in and continue to roll up.

Method

- Combine beef and shrimps and mix well.
- Heat two-thirds of the cooking oil and sauté onion and garlic. Add beef and shrimp mixture. Stir-fry until slightly dry.
- Add groundnuts, cilantro roots, pepper, fish sauce and sugar. Fry until meat is slightly dry. Set aside.

- Heat some of the remaining cooking oil and sprinkle beaten egg by hand in criss-cross lines to resemble a net. Make each net approximately 4 in (10 cm) in diameter. Lift the egg nets out with a wok ladle or spatula. Continue until all the egg is used up.

- Assemble each cutlet by placing 1 heaped Tbsp of cooked beef and shrimp mixture, a few cilantro leaves and red chilli strips on each egg net. Enclose ingredients with egg net. Continue until ingredients are used up.
- Serve garnished with cucumber, scallion and carrot.

PATTAYA-STYLE CHILLI FRIED BEEF

A spicy dish of Chinese mushrooms, beef, onion, bell pepper and bamboo shoots. Remove the seeds from the red chillies and reduce or omit the bird's eye chillies for a milder dish.

Ingredients

Groundnut oil	3 Tbsp
Dried Chinese mushrooms	10, soaked and finely sliced
Beef tenderloin	1 lb (500 g), finely sliced
Oyster sauce	2 Tbsp
Sugar	1 Tbsp
Fish sauce *(nam pla)*	3 Tbsp
Onion	1, peeled and sliced in rounds
Green bell pepper	1/4, cut into cubes
Red bell pepper	1/4, cut into cubes
Canned sour bamboo shoots	5 oz (140 g), sliced
Thai sweet basil *(bai horapa)* leaves	a handful
Cornstarch	1 tsp, mixed with 1 Tbsp water

Paste

Red chillies	4
Bird's eye chillies	8
Garlic	3 cloves, peeled

Garnish

Scallion	1, chopped

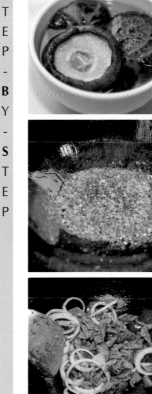

STEP-BY-STEP

To soften dried Chinese mushrooms in a hurry, soak them in warm water.

Stir-fry the paste in very hot oil so that the ingredients cook rather than absorb the oil.

Turn the ingredients over quickly in the wok to cook them evenly.

Method

- Combine paste ingredients and pound into a fine paste. Heat oil and fry the finely pounded paste until fragrant.
- Add mushrooms and stir-fry until soft. Add beef, oyster sauce, sugar and fish sauce and stir-fry for another 3 minutes.
- Add onion, green and red bell peppers, bamboo shoots and basil leaves. Pour in the cornstarch mixture and stir for a few minutes.
- Garnish with scallion and serve immediately.

Hold the lemon grass firmly in one hand and a sharp cleaver in the other hand to slice it finely in rounds.

Incorporate the coconut milk into the paste by stirring as you pour it in gradually.

Stir-fry the curry to heat through so the oil will separate from the ingredients.

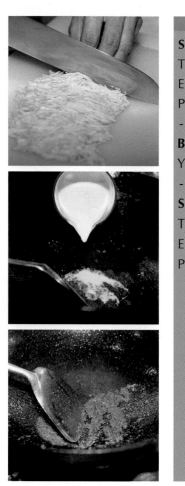

THAI PINEAPPLE SHRIMP CURRY

A spicy shrimp curry sweetened with the addition of pineapple.

Ingredients

Cooking oil	3 Tbsp
Coconut milk	2 cups (500 ml)
Kaffir lime leaves	3
Fish sauce *(nam pla)*	2 Tbsp
Salt	to taste
Sugar	to taste
Pineapple	³/₄ lb (350 g), sliced
Freshwater shrimps	1¹/₂ lb (700 g), medium-sized, legs and feelers removed
Thai sweet basil *(bai horapa)* leaves	a handful

Paste

Red chillies	10
Lemon grass	2 stalks, finely sliced
Galangal	¹/₂ in (1 cm) knob, peeled
Cilantro leaves	3 sprigs
Kaffir lime leaves	2 tsp, chopped
Black peppercorns	10
Ground cumin	2 tsp
Dried shrimp paste *(kapi)*	1 tsp
Ground turmeric	2 tsp

Method

- Combine paste ingredients and grind until fine.
- Heat oil and sauté finely ground paste until fragrant. Stir in coconut milk.
- Add kaffir lime leaves, fish sauce, salt, sugar and pineapple. Simmer until the oil starts separating.
- Add shrimps and basil leaves and simmer for 3 minutes.

Pull off the shell of the crab, remove the lungs and clean before cutting it in half down the middle.

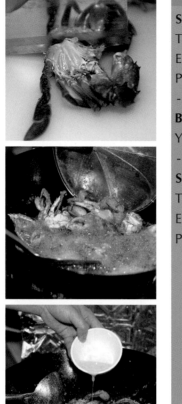

The crabs are cooked once the shells turn red.

Stir in the beaten egg quickly so that it is well mixed with the crabs and does not become an omelette.

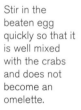

SPICY TOM YAM FRIED CRAB

Crabs cooked in an aromatic mixture of tom yam paste and bird's eye chillies.

Ingredients

Crabs	4, large, cleaned and cut in half
Freshly cracked white pepper	to taste
Cornstarch	2 Tbsp
Eggs	2, beaten separately
Sugar	2 tsp
Cooking oil for deep-frying	
Butter	3 Tbsp
Shallots	4, peeled and finely chopped
Garlic	2 cloves, peeled and finely chopped
Ginger	1 Tbsp, peeled and finely chopped
Tom yam paste	2 Tbsp
Bird's eye chillies	6, finely sliced
Light soy sauce	1 Tbsp

Garnish

Cilantro leaves	a handful, chopped

Method

- Mix together crabs, pepper, cornstarch, 1 egg and 1 tsp sugar. Deep-fry crabs in hot oil. Drain and set aside.
- Heat butter and fry shallots, garlic, ginger and tom yam paste. Add chillies, fried crabs, soy sauce and remaining sugar.
- Quickly stir in remaining egg and cook until done.
- Garnish with cilantro leaves before serving.

THAI STEAMED FISH MOUSSE

A popular Thai dish of steamed spicy fish paste. Serve hot as part of a main meal.

Ingredients

Coconut milk	2 cups (500 ml)
Rice flour	1 tsp
Spanish mackerel	1¼ lb (600 g), deboned and minced (ground)
Egg	1, beaten
Fish sauce (nam pla)	2 Tbsp
Sugar	1 tsp
Thai sweet basil (bai horapa)	1 sprig
Kaffir lime leaves	3, finely sliced
Cilantro leaves	2 Tbsp, chopped
Red chilli	1, finely sliced in strips
Banana leaf cups	15–20, each about 3 in (7.5 cm) wide

Curry Spices

Dried chillies	5, seeded, soaked and drained
Shallots	7, peeled
Garlic	3 cloves, peeled
Galangal	2 Tbsp, peeled and finely sliced
Lemon grass	2 Tbsp finely sliced
Cilantro roots	1 Tbsp, chopped
Ground white pepper	1 tsp
Salt	1 tsp
Dried shrimp paste (kapi)	1 tsp

S T E P - B Y - S T E P

Make the banana leaf cups by cutting 4 in (10 cm) circles from banana leaves. Fold at four points of the circle and secure with toothpicks.

The coconut paste serves as a backdrop to bring out the color of the leaves and chilli strips.

Method

- Mix half the coconut milk with rice flour and cook over medium heat until it boils and forms a paste. Remove from heat and set aside.
- Combine curry spices and grind until fine. In a large mixing bowl, combine the ground curry spices with remaining coconut milk, mackerel, egg, fish sauce and sugar. Stir well.
- Line bottom of banana leaf cups with basil leaves then fill with fish mixture. Steam for 15–20 minutes.
- Remove from heat. Pour some coconut paste on each cup of fish mousse and sprinkle kaffir lime leaves, cilantro leaves and chilli strips over. Steam for another minute.

BATTER FRIED MUSSELS WITH EGG

A light dish of mussels that can be served as a snack or as part of a main meal. Substitute the mussels with cockles or oysters as desired.

Ingredients

Tapioca flour	5 oz (140 g), sifted
All-purpose flour	2 oz (70 g), sifted
Water	1¹/₂ cups (375 ml)
Mussels	¹/₂ lb (250 g), boiled, shelled and drained
Cooking oil	¹/₄ cup (60 ml)
Garlic	1 oz (30 g), peeled, sliced and crisp-fried
Eggs	6
Fish sauce (nam pla)	¹/₃ cup (90 ml)
Sugar	3 oz (90 g)
Bean sprouts	10 oz (300 g), tailed
Cilantro leaves	2 sprigs, cut into 1 in (2.5 cm) lengths
Scallions	2, cut into 1 in (2.5 cm) lengths

Sauce

Red chillies	3, finely sliced
Sugar	1 Tbsp
Salt	1 tsp
Vinegar	¹/₂ cup (125 ml)

When the mussels are cooked, the shells will open. Gently pull the mussels from the shells and discard shells.

To avoid accidentally dropping any bit of egg shell into the batter, crack the egg into a bowl before pouring it onto the batter.

Scramble the mixture lightly and break the egg yolk.

Method

- Combine tapioca flour with all-purpose flour. Add water and mix into a batter. Divide into six portions.
- Divide mussels into six portions.
- Heat cooking oil and add 1 Tbsp of fried garlic and one portion each of mussels and batter.

- When batter begins to solidify, crack an egg on top. Sprinkle with 1 Tbsp fish sauce and 1 tsp sugar. Lightly scramble mixture with a spatula. Then add some bean sprouts, cilantro leaves and scallions. Cook until evenly brown and dish onto a serving plate. Repeat procedure until ingredients are used up.

- Combine sauce ingredients and blend. Serve mussels with the sauce.

SAVORY GOLDEN CUPS WITH SEAFOOD FILLING

An attractive appetizer of deep-fried spring roll wrappers filled with seafood, cashew nuts and button mushrooms.

Ingredients

Spring roll wrappers	6, cut into 3 in (7.5 cm) squares
Cooking oil for brushing	

Seafood Filling

Squid	5 oz (150 g), cleaned and finely diced
Tiger shrimps	7 oz (200 g), shelled, deveined and finely diced
Crabmeat	2 oz (50 g), shredded
Fish sauce (*nam pla*)	¼ cup (60 ml)
Cooking oil	⅓ cup (90 ml)
Cashew nuts	3 oz (100 g), coarsely chopped
Garlic	2 cloves, peeled and finely chopped
Red chilli	1, finely sliced
Kaffir lime leaves	2, torn into pieces
Canned button mushrooms	3 oz (100 g), finely sliced
Palm sugar (jaggery)	1 Tbsp, crushed or brown sugar
Lemon or lime juice	2 tsp
Cornstarch	1 Tbsp, blended with 2 Tbsp water

S-T-E-P - B-Y - S-T-E-P

Gently ease the spring roll wrappers into place with your fingers so that a lovely 'star' shape is formed.

Cut the shrimps and squid into dices of similar size so the resulting filling looks neat.

Canned button mushrooms are pre-cooked. Stir-fry them simply to heat them through.

Method

- Brush a sheet of spring roll wrapper with a little cooking oil and place another sheet over it so that an eight-sided 'star' is formed.
- Gently press it into a small fluted muffin tin or aluminum jelly mold. Hold it down by stacking with another tin/mold.
- Repeat with remaining spring roll wrappers.
- Transfer tins/molds onto a baking tray and bake in a preheated oven at 400° F (200° C) for 12–15 minutes or until light brown and crisp. Set aside.
- Marinate squid, shrimps and crabmeat in fish sauce for 5–10 minutes.

- Heat cooking oil and stir-fry cashew nuts until slightly brown. Drain and set aside.
- In the same oil, sauté garlic, chilli and kaffir lime leaves for 3 minutes. Add marinated seafood and mushrooms and stir-fry for 2–3 minutes.
- Add cashew nuts and mix well before adding palm sugar or brown sugar and lemon or lime juice. Stir in cornstarch mixture to thicken.
- To serve, spoon filling into baked spring roll cups and serve immediately.

Cut the crabs up into smaller pieces. This will allow the seasoning to penetrate into the flesh easily.

Reconstitute the glass noodles by soaking them in water at room temperature.

Stir the paste ingredients around quickly in the claypot to prevent them from burning.

S
T
E
P
-
B
Y
-
S
T
E
P

CRABS WITH GLASS NOODLES

This dish of crabs and glass noodles can be served as a complete meal on its own or with additional side dishes.

Ingredients

Crabs	1 lb (500 g), cleaned and cut into pieces
Cooking oil	3 Tbsp
Glass noodles	2 oz (55 g), soaked for 5 minutes and drained
Chicken stock (see recipe p.43)	1½ cups (375 ml)
Cilantro leaves	1 sprig, cut into ½ in (1 cm) lengths
Red chilli	1, seeded and cut into thin strips

Seasoning

Fish sauce (nam pla)	2 Tbsp
Sesame oil	2 Tbsp
Worcestershire sauce	1 Tbsp
Light soy sauce	1 Tbsp

Paste

Black peppercorns	1 Tbsp
Ginger	½ in (1 cm) knob, peeled
Cilantro roots	3, chopped
Garlic	3 cloves, peeled

Method

- Combine seasoning ingredients and blend (process). Marinate crabs in seasoning for 30 minutes.
- Combine paste ingredients and grind into a fine paste.

- Heat cooking oil in a claypot and fry finely ground paste for 5 minutes or until fragrant. Add marinated crabs, glass noodles and chicken stock. Stir well.
- Cover claypot and simmer for 8 minutes. Garnish with cilantro leaves and chilli strips. Serve hot.

Cut the banana leaves and aluminum foil into rectangles using a pair of kitchen scissors.

The kaffir lime leaves and chilli strips are placed first so they will be visible when the parcel is opened.

Carefully cut through the foil into the banana leaf using a small sharp knife.

BAKED SEAFOOD WRAPPED IN BANANA LEAF

A succulent dish of seafood lightly grilled to perfection.

Ingredients

Banana leaf	
Aluminum foil	
Kaffir lime leaves	5, finely sliced
Red chillies	2, cut into fine strips
Seafood filling (see recipe p.75)	
Mussels	3 oz (100 g), shelled and boiled
Cabbage	1/2 lb (250 g), shredded and blanched
Thai sweet basil (bai horapa)	2 sprigs, stalks removed

Garnish

Lettuce leaves	2, sliced
Scallion	1, chopped
Carrot	1, peeled and sliced
Lemon	1, cut into wedges

Method

- Cut banana leaf and aluminum foil into 6 x 8 in (15 x 20 cm) rectangles. Place banana leaf on top of aluminium foil.
- Layer sliced kaffir lime leaves and red chilli strips in the middle of the banana leaf. Add 3 Tbsp of the seafood filling, 3 mussels, cabbage and basil leaves. Top with another 1 Tbsp of the seafood filling and form into a square parcel.
- Bake or grill (broil) parcels for 20 minutes.
- To serve, cut open the foil and banana leaf to resemble a flower. Garnish with lettuce leaves, scallion and carrot. Serve with lemon wedges.

SEAFOOD FILLING

Ingredients

Boiled coconut cream	1 portion (see page 27)
Shrimps	3 oz (100 g), small, shelled and deveined
Crabmeat	3 oz (100 g), shredded
Fish fillet	3 oz (100 g), cut into 1 in (2.5 cm) pieces
Fish sauce *(nam pla)*	2 Tbsp
Palm sugar *(jaggery)*	1 Tbsp, crushed or brown sugar
Eggs	2, beaten

Paste

Red chillies	10, seeded
Galangal	1½ in (3.5 cm) knob, peeled
Lemon grass	3 stalks, sliced
Shallots	6, peeled
Garlic	15 cloves, peeled
Cilantro root	1, chopped
Dried shrimp paste *(kapi)*	½ in (1 cm) piece
Lesser ginger *(kra chai)*	1 tsp, peeled and chopped

Method

- Combine paste ingredients and grind until fine and pasty.
- Heat boiled coconut cream for 5 minutes. Add finely ground paste and cook until fragrant.
- Add shrimps, crabmeat, fish, fish sauce, palm sugar or brown sugar. Stir.
- Remove from heat and add in beaten egg. Mix well and use as needed.

STUFFED CRABS

Crab shells stuffed with a seasoned minced pork mixture, then steamed to seal in the juices and deep-fried to achieve an attractive golden color.

Ingredients

Garlic	1 Tbsp, peeled and chopped
Cilantro root	1 Tbsp, chopped
Black peppercorns	10
Shallots	2, peeled and chopped
Fish sauce *(nam pla)*	1 Tbsp (15 ml)
Pork	7 oz (200 g), minced (ground)
Cooked or canned crabmeat	1 lb (500 g), mashed
Cilantro leaves	4–6 sprigs
Egg yolks	2
Cooking oil for deep-frying	
Crab shells	4–6

STEP-BY-STEP

Pound the ingredients using a mortar and pestle.

Press the meat mixture tightly into the crab shells with wet hands so the mixture will not stick to your hands.

Lower the crab shells gently into the hot oil to avoid splattering.

Method

- Pound together garlic, cilantro root, peppercorns and onion with the fish sauce. Mix in pork then knead in mashed crabmeat.
- Fill crab shells with this mixture. Place in a steamer over boiling water and steam for 15 minutes, then top with cilantro leaves and coat with egg yolk.

- Heat enough oil to deep-fry stuffed shells. When oil is hot, drop in stuffed shells, and cook until tops turn brown. Serve with Thai chilli sauce if desired.

VEGETABLES & SALADS

Choose ripe but firm tomatoes so they do not dent under pressure. Scoop the center out of the tomato using a melon baller or teaspoon.

Stuff the tomatoes tightly so they hold their shape when baked.

You can make the egg nets using your fingers or a sieve.

S
T
E
P
-
B
Y
-
S
T
E
P

CRAB AND PORK STUFFED TOMATOES

A colorful dish of stuffed tomatoes wrapped in egg net.

Ingredients

Tomatoes	10
Salt	to taste
Cilantro roots	3, chopped
Garlic	4 cloves, peeled and chopped
Black peppercorns	10
Pork	½ lb (250 g), minced (ground)
Cooked or canned crabmeat	½ lb (250 g)
Onion	1, peeled and chopped
Sugar	1 tsp
Fish sauce (nam pla)	2 Tbsp
Eggs	5, beaten

Method

- Slice tops off tomatoes and set aside to be used as lids. Scoop out tomato flesh and coat inside of tomato shells lightly with salt. Stand upside down to allow excess water to drain.
- Pound together cilantro roots, garlic and peppercorns. Mix in pork, crab, onion, sugar, fish sauce and 1 egg.
- Rinse and dry tomato shells. Stuff with the mixture and cover with reserved lids.
- Cook in a preheated oven at 350° F (180° C) for 30 minutes.
- Use remaining eggs (see recipe p.57) to make egg nets.
- Roll cooked, stuffed tomatoes in egg nets. Serve with a sauce of your choice.

Slice the scallops off the shells using a paring knife.

Cut the lettuce leaves to size so they fit nicely on a scallop shell without obscuring it completely.

SCALLOP SALAD

This light and refreshing scallop dish is not only attractive to the eye, but also tasty. Serve as a starter or side dish.

Ingredients

Scallops with shells	9
Lettuce	1 head
Onion	1 large, peeled and finely sliced
Cilantro leaves	5 sprigs, coarsely chopped (optional)

Dressing

Lemon juice	2 Tbsp
Garlic	2 cloves, peeled and crushed
Bird's eye chillies	2, crushed
Salt	to taste
Olive oil	1 Tbsp
Whole red chillies (optional)	to taste

Method

- Buy scallops already opened. Remove from shells and discard black beards and intestines. Wash well, then place in a saucepan of cold water. Bring to simmering point, skim, and cook gently for 5–10 minutes.

- Meanwhile, wash shells and line with leaves taken from the heart of the lettuce. Slice cooked scallops or leave whole and arrange on the lettuce with sliced onion and coarsely chopped cilantro, if using.

- Mix dressing ingredients together thoroughly, adding as many whole chillies as you like, or none at all if you prefer. Serve dressing on the side or pour over scallops.

PAPAYA SALAD

The sourness of the raw papaya makes this salad an ideal way to cleanse the palate and excite the taste buds before or during a meal.

Ingredients

Raw papaya	4–5 cups (1–1.25 liters), peeled and coarsely grated
Garlic	3 cloves, peeled and chopped
Bird's eye chilies	3, chopped
Fish sauce *(nam pla)*	1 Tbsp
Lemon juice	2 Tbsp
Groundnuts	2 Tbsp, crushed
Ground white pepper	to taste
Lettuce and cabbage leaves	

Garnish

Tomatoes	3, thinly sliced

STEP-BY-STEP

Grate the papaya using a handheld grater. Be careful not to grate your fingers as the papaya thins.

Crush the groundnuts with a mortar and pestle or in a sealed plastic bag with a roller.

Toss the salad with tongs to mix well.

Method

- Mix grated papaya with garlic, chillies, fish sauce, lemon juice and groundnuts. Season with pepper.
- Serve on a bed of lettuce and cabbage leaves. Garnish with tomato slices.

THAI MUSHROOM CURRY

A spicy oyster mushroom curry that goes well with white rice. For a milder curry, use fewer or omit the bird's eye chillies completely when making the paste.

Ingredients

Cooking oil	$^1/_3$ cup (90 ml)
Fresh oyster mushrooms	1 lb (500 g)
Water	$1^3/_4$ cup (435 ml)
Kaffir lime leaves	4
Polygonum leaves	1 stalk
Red bird's eye chillies	10
Coconut milk	2 cups (500 ml)
Fish sauce (nam pla)	$2^1/_2$ Tbsp
Salt	2 tsp
Ground white pepper	$^1/_2$ tsp

Paste

Green chillies	4
Bird's eye chillies	20
Shallots	8, peeled
Garlic	5 cloves, peeled
Cilantro roots	2
Kaffir lime rind	grated from 1 small lime
Ground cumin	$2^1/_2$ tsp
Lemon grass	4 stalks, finely sliced
Galangal	$^1/_2$ in (1 cm) knob, peeled and sliced
Dried shrimp paste (kapi)	$^1/_2$ in (1 cm) square

STEP-BY-STEP

Carefully peel the galangal with a paring knife. Wipe with a damp cloth before slicing.

Stir in the mushrooms, making sure that they are well-coated with the curry gravy.

Add in the final ingredients and simmer until the curry is of your preferred consistency.

Method

- Combine paste ingredients and grind into a fine paste. Heat oil and sauté finely ground paste until fragrant.
- Stir in mushrooms and water. Bring to the boil for 10 minutes.

- Add kaffir lime leaves, polygonum leaves and bird's eye chillies. Stir in coconut milk, fish sauce, salt and pepper. Simmer for another 10 minutes and serve hot.

Arrange the asparagus spears in a row and slice to get even lengths.

Sauté the lemon grass, garlic and ginger until fragrant and the garlic is just lightly browned.

The time taken for the asparagus to become tender will depend on the size of the spears. Stir in a little water if the mixture becomes too dry.

ASPARAGUS IN COCONUT CREAM AND LEMON GRASS SAUCE

Stir-fried asparagus and shrimps in a creamy coconut sauce.

Ingredients

Cooking oil	2 Tbsp
Lemon grass	2 stalks, finely sliced
Garlic	2 cloves, peeled and finely sliced
Young ginger	$3/4$ in (1.5 cm) knob, peeled and finely sliced
Asparagus spears	1 lb (500 g), cut into $2^1/2$ in (5 cm) lengths
Shrimps	5 oz (150 g), shelled and deveined
Coconut milk	1 cup (250 ml)
Bean sprouts	$1/2$ lb (250 g), tailed, blanched and drained

Garnish

Red chilli	1, finely sliced

Method

- Heat cooking oil and fry lemon grass, garlic and ginger until fragrant.
- Add asparagus, shrimps and coconut milk and bring to the boil. Simmer for 5 minutes or until asparagus is tender.
- Arrange blanched bean sprouts on a serving plate, top with asparagus and garnish with red chilli slices.

Wash the fish then make a slit in the belly. Remove the guts using your fingers. Rinse well.

Use a fork to flake the flesh off the fish. Have it chunkier if you prefer.

Halve and core the apple, then slice finely. Do this just before making the salad or the apple may oxidize and brown.

SPICY MACKEREL SALAD

A light but tasty fried fish salad with crushed chillies, groundnuts and green apple strips.

Ingredients

Mackerels	4, medium, gutted and cleaned
Cooking oil for frying	
Shallots	4–5, peeled and chopped
Ginger	1 in (2.5 cm) knob, peeled and grated
Red chillies	4, lightly crushed
Green chillies	4, lightly crushed
Groundnuts	3 Tbsp, crushed
Green apple	1/2, cut into fine strips
Lemon juice	3 Tbsp
Lemon rind	1 Tbsp, grated
Salt	to taste
Freshly ground black pepper	to taste
Lettuce leaves	5

Garnish
Cilantro leaves

Method

- Steam fish for 5–7 minutes. Before they are completely cooked, remove fish from steamer and lightly pat dry.
- Heat cooking oil and fry steamed fish until golden. Drain and leave to cool. Debone and skin, then flake the flesh.
- In a bowl, mix fish meat with shallots, ginger, chillies, groundnuts and apple. Add lemon juice and rind. Season with salt and pepper. Mix well.
- Dish out onto a plate lined with lettuce leaves. Garnish with cilantro leaves.

KIDNEY BEAN SALAD

A nutritious salad of kidney beans and firm bean curd strips.

Ingredients

Chilli powder	1/2 tsp
Shallot	1 Tbsp, peeled and chopped
Garlic	1 Tbsp, peeled and crushed
Galangal	1 tsp, peeled and chopped
Lemon grass	1 tsp, finely sliced
Salt	1 tsp
Cooking oil	2 Tbsp
Firm bean curd	1/2 piece, cut into strips
Canned kidney beans	10 oz (300 g), drained
Vegetable stock	3 Tbsp (see page 31)
Lemon juice	1 Tbsp
Light soy sauce	1 Tbsp
Lettuce	1/2 head
Chinese cabbage	1 head

Garnish

Cilantro leaves	1 Tbsp, chopped
Mint leaves	1 Tbsp, chopped
Cucumber	1, sliced

S T E P - B Y - S T E P

Peel the galangal and wipe with a damp cloth. Slice and chop the required amount for the recipe.

Fry the pounded ingredients until fragrant before adding in the bean curd, kidney beans and stock.

Keep tossing the ingredients so the liquid will evaporate faster, but be careful not to break the bean curd strips or kidney beans.

Method

- Pound together chilli powder, shallot, garlic, galangal, lemon grass and salt.
- Heat oil and fry pounded ingredients. Add bean curd, kidney beans and stock. Keep frying until liquid reduces and mixture is dry.
- Remove from heat. Add lemon juice and soy sauce and mix well. Allow to cool.
- When cold, serve kidney bean salad on a thick bed of lettuce and cabbage leaves. Garnish with cilantro, mint and cucumber.

Squeeze out the excess water from the mushrooms before chopping. Otherwise the water will soak through the spring roll wrappers and break them.

To create the pouch, bring the edges of the spring roll wrappers to the center with both hands.

Gently lower the pouches into the hot oil with your fingers or use a wire strainer.

THAI MONEY BAGS

Deep-fried pouches of diced chicken, Chinese mushrooms, water chestnuts, shrimps and glass noodles.

Ingredients

Cooking oil	$^1/_4$ cup (60 ml) + more for deep-frying
Garlic	4 cloves, peeled and finely chopped
Boneless chicken	7 oz (200 g), finely diced
Oyster sauce	2 Tbsp
Light soy sauce	1 tsp
Ground white pepper	$^1/_2$ tsp
Sesame oil	$^1/_2$ tsp
Dried Chinese mushrooms	6, soaked in hot water and finely chopped
Water chestnuts	6, peeled and finely diced
Shrimps	7 oz (200 g), small, shelled and deveined
Glass noodles	2 oz (55 g), soaked in hot water and drained
Scallions	2, finely chopped
Cornstarch	1 tsp, mixed with 1 Tbsp water
Spring roll wrappers	10–12 sheets, each about 4 x 4 in (10 x 10 cm)
Dried scallions	10–12

Method

- To make the filling, heat oil and add garlic, chicken, oyster sauce, soy sauce, pepper and sesame oil. Sauté until chicken is cooked. Add mushrooms, water chestnuts and shrimps and cook for 1 minute.
- Add glass noodles and chopped scallions. Mix well. Stir in cornstarch mixture and cook until sauce is thick. Leave to cool.
- Take a sheet of spring roll wrapper and top with 4 tsp filling. Bring the edges of the spring roll wrapper together and secure with a length of scallion to resemble a small pouch. Neaten pouch top with a pair of scissors. Repeat until ingredients are used up.
- Heat oil for deep-frying and fry pouches until golden brown. Drain. Serve hot with Thai chilli sauce.

Introduce the water gradually to the flour. Mix well before adding more water each time.

Tie the cloth tightly over the mouth of the saucepan so it acts as a sturdy work surface to steam the rice pancakes.

Ease the pancake from the cloth using a palette knife. Wet the knife before using so the pancake does not stick to it.

STEP-BY-STEP

STEAMED RICE PANCAKES WITH PORK

A light snack of steamed rice flour pancakes with a savory filling.

Ingredients

Pancake Batter

Rice flour	1½ cup (325 ml)
Tapioca flour	¼ cup (60 ml)
Water	1¾ cup (450 ml)

Filling

Cooking oil	2 Tbsp
Garlic	1 Tbsp, peeled and crushed
Cilantro root	1 Tbsp, chopped
Ground white pepper	1 tsp
Pork	7 oz (200 g), minced or ground
Palm sugar (jaggery)	3 Tbsp
Fish sauce (nam pla)	2 Tbsp
Turnip	¼ lb (125 g), peeled and grated
Water	¼ cup (60 ml)
Shallots	1, peeled and finely sliced
Groundnuts	2 oz (50 g), crushed
Cilantro leaves	

Method

- Mix rice and tapioca flour with water to produce pancake batter. Set aside.
- For the filling, heat oil and brown crushed garlic and cilantro root. Add pepper and pork and sauté for 3–4 minutes until browned. Remove pork mixture and reserve.
- In the same frying pan (skillet), mix palm sugar, fish sauce, turnip and water. Bring to the boil and stir until mixture boils down and becomes drier. Add cooked pork mixture, onion and groundnuts and mix well. Cook for another 5 minutes. Remove from heat.

- The only successful way to cook rice pancakes is by steaming. Half fill a fairly deep, flameproof container or saucepan with water. Stretch a piece of muslin or cotton over the top like a drum and tie down tightly with string. Place over medium heat. When steam appears through the material, spread a fine layer of batter over it. Cover with a lid for 1 minute to cook pancake.
- Place 1 Tbsp of pork mixture in the center of pancake. Top with cilantro leaves, then fold sides of pancake over to form a square parcel.
- Repeat with remaining batter and pork mixture.

COCONUT BANANAS

A sweet dessert of boiled bananas served with warm coconut cream.

Ingredients:

Bananas	6–9
Water	2 cups (500 ml)
Sugar	3/4 lb (350 g)
Coconut cream	1/2 cup (125 ml)
Salt	1/2 tsp

STEP-BY-STEP

Bring the water and sugar to the boil, stirring. Watch the pot so that it does not boil over.

Slip the bananas gently into the syrup one by one. Once they take on a darker shade of yellow, they are cooked and ready.

Stir the coconut cream as it boils to help it thicken.

Method

- Peel bananas. If they are large, cut in half across, but if they are small, leave whole.
- Mix water with sugar, and bring to the boil, stirring. Simmer for 5 minutes. Add bananas and cook for 5 minutes. Drain.
- Bring coconut cream to the boil with salt. Reduce heat and stir until liquid thickens.
- Serve bananas with warm coconut cream.

Cut the long beans diagonally into thin slices so it complements the texture of the fishcake perfectly.

Mix the ingredients until they are well-combined as a soft dough.

Press the dough into a neat pattie so that it holds together well and does not break up when fried.

SPICY RED CURRY FISH CAKE

A light and tasty deep-fried fish cake of minced fish and red curry paste.

Ingredients

Red curry paste (see recipe p.47)	5 oz (140 g)
Red snapper fillet	1 lb (500 g), minced (ground)
Egg	1, small
Fish sauce (nam pla)	3 Tbsp
Cilantro leaves	1 sprig, chopped
Palm sugar (jaggery)	1 Tbsp, crushed or brown sugar
Long beans	3 oz (80 g), thinly sliced
Cooking oil	3 cups (750 ml)
Special chilli sauce (see recipe p.103)	

Method

- Combine red curry paste and fish with egg, fish sauce, cilantro leaves, palm sugar or brown sugar and long beans. Knead into a soft dough.
- Shape 2 Tbsp of dough into a ball and flatten slightly. Deep-fry fish cakes until golden brown. Drain. Serve with special chilli sauce.

SPECIAL CHILLI SAUCE

Ingredients

Sugar	7 oz (200 g)
Salt	2 tsp
Vinegar	1/2 cup (125 ml)
Water	2 Tbsp
Garlic	5 cloves, peeled and finely ground
Red chillies	2, finely ground
Shallots	3, peeled and sliced
Cucumber	1, quartered lengthways and thinly sliced
Roasted groundnuts	3 Tbsp, pounded

Method

- Boil sugar, salt, vinegar and water until sugar is dissolved.
- Add garlic, red chillies, shallots, cucumber slices, groundnuts and mix well.

Stir the coconut milk and glutinous rice mixture as it boils so it does not burn and will be evenly cooked.

Spoon the glutinous rice onto the center of the banana leaf so it is easy to fold into a neat parcel.

Thread the toothpick through the banana leaf, being careful not to prick your finger or tear the leaf.

S
T
E
P
-
B
Y
-
S
T
E
P

STEAMED GLUTINOUS RICE WITH BANANA AND KIDNEY BEANS

Sticky glutinous rice topped with banana slices and boiled kidney beans, sealed in a banana leaf parcel.

Ingredients

Coconut milk	3 cups (750 ml)
Salt	1 tsp
Sugar	¼ lb (125 g)
Glutinous rice	1 lb (450 g), washed, soaked for 3–4 hours and drained
Semi-ripe bananas	2, peeled and finely sliced
Kidney beans	¼ lb (125 g), washed and boiled until soft
Banana leaves	5, cut into 4 x 6 in (10 x 15 cm) pieces
Bamboo toothpicks	10

Method

- Combine coconut milk with salt and sugar and stir well until sugar has dissolved. Strain coconut milk through a muslin cloth.
- Bring to the boil and add glutinous rice. Stir constantly over medium heat until liquid is absorbed. Remove from heat and set aside to cool.

- Place 1 Tbsp of glutinous rice on a piece of banana leaf and flatten rice slightly. Layer with a few slices of banana, another tablespoonful of glutinous rice and some kidney beans. Fold up the lengths of the banana leaf to enclose the filling. Secure the two open ends with toothpicks. Repeat until ingredients are used up.

- Steam parcels over rapidly boiling water for 20–25 minutes. Serve hot or cold.

Make four cuts at regular intervals along one side of the leaf, up to the spine. Fold at these notches to create a square case. Trim off any excess leaf.

The cooked arrowroot mixture should take on a translucent color.

Use a container with a spout to facilitate pouring the coconut cream into the screwpine leaf cases.

WATER CHESTNUT CAKE WITH COCONUT CREAM TOPPING

A crunchy dessert of crunchy water chestnut cake with a rich coconut cream topping.

Ingredients

Arrowroot flour	5 heaped Tbsp, sifted
Screwpine leaf (bay toey) juice (see recipe p.107)	3 Tbsp
Water	3 cups (750 ml)
Sugar	$^1/_2$ lb (220 g)
Water chestnuts	12, peeled and finely diced
Screwpine leaf (bay toey) cases	30

Coconut Cream Topping

Coconut milk	$2^1/_2$ cups (625 ml)
Rice flour	2 Tbsp, sifted
Cornstarch	1 Tbsp, sifted
Salt	$^1/_2$ tsp

Method

- Combine arrowroot flour, screwpine leaf juice, water and sugar in a pan and cook until thick and shiny. Add in chestnuts and mix well. Pour into screwpine leaf cases until they are half-full. Set in the refrigerator for about 30 minutes.

- Meanwhile prepare the coconut cream topping. Cook coconut milk with rice flour, cornstarch and salt until thick.
- Fill screwpine leaf cases with coconut cream topping and leave aside to cool before serving.

SCREWPINE LEAF JUICE

Ingredients

Screwpine leaves *(bay toey)*	10
Water	3 Tbsp

Method

- Cut screwpine leaves crosswise into 1 in (2.5 cm) lengths. Pound leaves, add water and squeeze to extract juice. Strain juice through a muslin cloth.

POMEGRANATE SEEDS IN COCONUT MILK

A brightly-colored dessert of diced water chestnuts covered in a translucent coating, and served in sweetened coconut milk.

Ingredients

Water chestnuts	10 oz (300 g), peeled and finely diced
Red food coloring	1 tsp, dissolved in 1 cup (250 ml) water
Tapioca flour	2 oz (60 g), sifted
Cornstarch	2 Tbsp, sifted
Water	5 cups (1.25 liters)

Coconut Syrup

Sugar	5 oz (150 g)
Water	1 cup (250 ml)
Screwpine leaves *(bay tocy)*	2, shredded and knotted
Coconut milk	1¼ cup (300 ml)

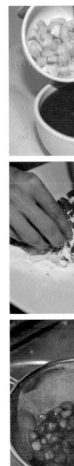

STEP-BY-STEP

Allow enough time for the water chestnuts to soak in the colored water so that an attractive red color can be achieved.

Coat the water chestnut cubes thoroughly in flour by mixing with clean, dry fingers.

Wash the cooked water chestnut cubes under running water to remove excess starch and prevent them from sticking together.

Method

- Soak water chestnut cubes in colored water until they turn red.
- Combine tapioca flour and cornstarch. Roll water chestnut cubes in flour to coat. Shake off excess flour.
- Bring water to the boil. Add coated water chestnut cubes and boil for 3 minutes. Remove and rinse under running water. Drain well.
- Wrap cooked water chestnut cubes in thin muslin cloth and set aside.
- Meanwhile, prepare coconut syrup. Boil sugar, water and screwpine leaves. Remove and set aside to cool. Add coconut milk and stir well.
- To serve, top water chestnut cubes with coconut syrup.

GLOSSARY OF INGREDIENTS

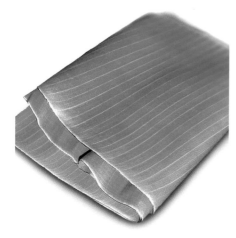

Banana Leaf
Banana leaves are not edible, but these broad green leaves are commonly used in Asia and in other tropical countries to wrap (or hold) and cook food. The banana leaves impart an aromatic quality to food. In Thai cooking, banana leaves are commonly cut and folded into small containers to steam or bake food. Such dishes are not only tasty, they are also very attractive to the eye.

Banana Blossom (Dok Kluai)
The banana blossom is found at the end of the banana fruit bunch, giving it its other common name of 'banana heart'. The tough outer layers must be peeled away to reveal the tender yellow part. Finely slice or cube this tender portion and flavor with spices or blanch and sprinkle with sauce before eating. The hard outer layers are sometimes reserved and cleaned for use as serving 'bowls'.

Bamboo Shoots
The tender, young shoots of the bamboo plant, bamboo shoots are harvested when they first appear at the base of the bamboo plant. The bamboo shoot is covered with dark colored leaves which should first be peeled off before use. Inside the flesh is cream-colored. Fresh bamboo shoots must be boiled for at least an hour before it is ready for use. After boiling, leave the shoots to soak in water until required. Bamboo shoots are available fresh, canned, pickled or sour.

Bell Peppers
The bell peppers used in Asian cooking are bell-shaped and sweet. They come in a variety of colors, from green and yellow to red. They do not vary significantly in taste, but the yellow and green ones are comparatively sweeter to the red ones which can sometimes taste a little 'spicy'. Choose bell peppers that are heavy, firm and glossy. Avoid the ones that are starting to wrinkle or are bruised. Good bell peppers are crunchy and juicy. Slice the bell peppers in half and remove the white core and seeds. Then slice as desired or recommended in the recipe.

Chilli

Several varieties of chillies are used in Thai cooking. Of the fresh chillies, there are the red ones (ripe chillies), the green ones (unripe chillies) and the bird's eye chillies (small chillies that are extremely spicy). The dried variety is made from drying red chillies. Soak dried chillies in warm water for at least 20 minutes to soften before use. Adjust the number and/or amount of fresh or dried chillies added to a dish to suit your preference. The general rule of thumb is that the smaller the chilli, the spicier it is. Deseeding chillies, whether fresh or dried, will also help make dishes less spicy. Wear gloves when cutting or slicing fresh chillies, as direct contact may leave a 'burning' sensation on your skin. Wash your hands thoroughly with soap and water after contact with fresh chillies, and do not touch your eyes or other sensitive areas of your body. Put chillies in a blender with a small amount of water to get chilli paste.

Coconut Cream/Milk

Coconut cream/milk is a common ingredient used in Thai cooking, in dishes such as curries and desserts, and also beverages. Coconut cream is thicker and richer than coconut milk. It is extracted by soaking fresh grated coconut in a small amount of water and then straining it in a fine sieve or muslin bag. Vary the thickness of the coconut cream/milk according to your preference. Ready-made versions are now available from markets and supermarkets for added convenience. Add water as desired to dilute the liquid.

Cornstarch

This flour has a bleached-white color which distinguishes it from all-purpose flour. It is obtained from the endosperm of the corn kernel and has no smell or flavor. Cornstarch is commonly used as a thickener for sauces and gravies and to bind meat mixtures. As it tends to form lumps, mix cornstarch with a small amount of liquid to form a thin paste before stirring into hot liquids. Sauces and gravies that are thickened with cornstarch are clear instead of opaque as with other flour-based sauces and gravies.

Cilantro

Also known as Chinese parsley and coriander, cilantro is fully edible, from its leaves to its stems and roots. The attractive bright green colored leaves are commonly used to garnish dishes as well as to flavor foods. When storing cilantro, first pat them dry with absorbent paper or kitchen towel, then wrap in clean absorbent paper or keep in an airtight container. Refrigerate and use as needed. Cilantro will keep for up to a week this way, depending on the freshness of the herb.

Dried Egg Noodles

These yellow colored noodles are thin like angel hair pasta. A main ingredient is egg, which is what gives it its rich yellow colour. These dried noodles can be reconstituted quickly by blanching in boiling water for 2–3 minutes. When reconstituted, they take on a light springy texture. Do no soak in water for too long as the noodles will absorb the water and lose their springy texture.

Dried Shrimps

These are small shrimps that have been completely shelled and then salted and sun-dried. Dried shrimps add flavor to dishes. They can be used whole, chopped or finely ground. Simply rinse or if preferred, soak in water for 10–15 minutes to remove the salty flavor.

Fish Sauce (Nam Pla)

This sauce is made from a brew of fermented fish or shrimps, and ranges in color from light brown to dark brown. Salty, pungent and strong-flavored, fish sauce is commonly used in Southeast Asia to enhance the flavor of dishes. Just as with soy sauce, fish sauce is used either as a condiment or added to food during cooking. As a condiment, it is sometimes served together with sliced chillies and/or lime juice.

Galangal

This rhizome looks like ginger, but it can be distinguished from the former by its faint pinkish colour. Galangal has a distinctive peppery taste that is best when fresh. It lends a unqiue flavor to the dish when used in cooking. The flesh is cream-colored. Slice off the required amount and peel off the skin before using. The remaining root can then be stored for later use. Simply slice off the dried portion.

Glass Noodles

Also known as cellophane noodles or bean vermicelli, these thin, dried transparent noodles can be softened in warm water before use or simply placed in boiling water to cook until tender. Glass noodles do not have much flavor of their own. As such, they take on the flavor of the gravy or soup they are cooked in most readily.

Glutinous Rice

Unlike other types of rice, this variety of rice is opaque white in color. Soak the rice in water for at least 3 hours or preferably overnight before cooking. When cooked, glutinous rice takes on a sticky texture, as with Japanese rice. Allow less rice for each person when cooking glutinous rice, as it is more filling compared to other types of rice. In Thai cooking, glutinous rice is commonly used to prepare desserts and snacks.

Kaffir Lime

This knobbly, dark green colored lime has a very fragrant rind that is commonly used to flavor curries and soups in Thai cooking. Its leaves are also dark green in color and look like two leaves joined end to end. Like the rind, they are also used to flavor curries and soups. Shred or tear the leaves to release its strong fragrance.

Light Soy Sauce

A very common and almost essential ingredient used in Asian cooking, light soy sauce is made from fermented soy beans. Light soy sauce is clear, and light brown in color, with a salty taste. It is used to add flavor to dishes without darkening them as would be the case with dark soy sauce. Light soy sauce is commonly added to fish, meat, chicken, vegetable and soup dishes. It is also used as a condiment for dipping. Sliced chilli can be added to make the condiment spicier.

Lemon Grass

This is a very important herb in Thai cooking. With long thin light green-grey leaves and a bulbous base, only the lower 4–6 in (10–15 cm) portion of the herb is used in cooking. Fragrant and aromatic, lemon grass imparts a distinctive lemony flavor dishes. To use, trim off the base and peel off the tough outer layers to reveal the tender center. Bruise to release its flavor when the herb is used whole, or slice finely.

Mushrooms

Both dried and fresh mushrooms are used in Thai cooking, but the dried Chinese mushrooms (dried shiitake mushrooms) are used most frequently. Soak dried Chinese mushrooms in warm water for at least 20 minutes to soften. Squeeze out the excess liquid before using. Dried Chinese mushrooms are available from Chinese supermarkets or specialty stores. Canned button mushrooms are used in some Thai recipes. Do not substitute with the fresh variety, as they taste rather different. Drain well and use as required.

Palm Sugar (Jaggery)

Made from the sap of the coconut or palm trees, this natural sugar varies in color from dark to light brown. It is less sweet than cane sugar and has a distinctive fragrance and flavor. Palm sugar has a soft texture and may melt easily depending on where it is stored. Store in a cool dark place in an airtight container. Palm sugar usually comes in a cylindrical block or in rounds. If unavailable, substitute with brown sugar.

Lesser Ginger (Kra Chai)

Lesser ginger comes in bunches of slender, short turberous roots. They range in colour from yellow to light brown and have a distinct aromatic flavor. Omit it from the recipe if it is unavailable.

Shrimp Paste (Kapi)

Dried shrimp paste is fine-textured and strong-flavored. It is commonly used in Thai cooking, as well as in other Asian dishes. It varies in color from pink to dark brown. Unless otherwise specified in the recipe, grill, pan-fry or pound before using to get the best of its flavor. Another type of shrimp paste comes in the form of a thick dark colored liquid, with an equally pungent flavor. These two types of shrimp pastes have different uses and should not be used as substitutes for each other.

Preserved Soy Beans

Preserved soy beans are rather salty and have a unique flavor. They are added to dishes when cooking or used to make tasty sauces. The beans can be used whole or mashed to make a paste. When preserved soy beans are used in a dish, salt is commonly omitted or significantly reduced.

Rice Noodles (Thick or Thin)

Made from rice flour, these white rice noodles are available fresh from the market and supermarket. The thick and thin types differ only in the way they have been cut (broad or narrow). They are relatively bland on their own and they readily take on the flavor of the gravy or soup they are cooked in. These noodles have been pre-oiled to prevent them from sticking. Blanch lightly to remove excess oil if preferred, although this is not necessary.

Screwpine Leaf (Bai Toey)

Also known as pandan leaf, screwpine leaves are long and slender. They have a glossy dark green color and a stiff spine down the center of each leaf. The fragrant leaf is used to enhance the flavor of many Asian dishes. Meats and desserts wrapped in the leaf take on the subtle fragrance of the leaf. Essence of the screwpine leaf can also be extracted by blending the chopped leaf with a small amount of water and then straining with a fine sieve or muslin bag. The green color of the extract will also add an attractive light green tinge to dishes, especially desserts.

Scallion

This immature onion has a white undeveloped base and long thin green leaves. The leaves have a hollow center. Fully edible, scallions have a mild onion taste and are used in Asian cooking to add flavor and also color to dishes. Choose scallions with crisp, sturdy green leaves. To store, pat dry and wrap in clean absorbent paper in an airtight container or a clean plastic bag. Refrigerate for up to a week.

Shallots

Shallots are members of the onion family, but like garlic, a head of shallots is formed from multiple cloves. They have thin paper-like skin. In Asia, shallots are small to medium sized and have a reddish purple skin. Choose shallots that are plump and firm, not the wrinkled ones with signs of sprouting. Store in a cool, dry and well-ventilated place. Shallots are commonly peeled and then smashed, sliced or chopped and stir-fried in hot oil to get the best out of their flavor. Do not overcook, as they will brown quickly and become bitter.

Spring Roll Wrappers

These are thin dough wrappers available fresh or frozen. Defrost the frozen wrappers before use and cover with a damp cloth to prevent them from drying out.

Tamarind Pulp

Tamarind is used in many Thai dishes to impart a fragrant sour flavor to foods. Tamarind pulp is brown in color and is available in packet form, from the market and supermarket. To use, the required amount of tamarind pulp is first soaked in water for about 10 minutes. The liquid is then strained of any fibre and seeds to obtain the sour juice.

Tapioca Flour

Tapioca flour is commonly used to make Asian dessert and snacks. It is also used as a thickening agent for gravies, sauces and soups, much like cornstarch. If tapioca flour is not available, substitute with cornstarch.

Thai Sweet Basil (Bai Horapa)

Also known as sweet basil, this aromatic herb is used widely in Thai cooking. Whenever possible, use the herb fresh, as it does not retain its flavor when dried. When choosing Thai sweet basil, choose leaves with a fresh green color that show no sign of wilting. Add the whole leaves to dishes or slice them finely. To store, place the herb stem-down in a glass of water and refrigerate. Fresh Thai sweet basil will keep for up to a few days.

Tom Yam Paste

This traditional Thai soup base is spicy and sour at the same time. It is made from a mixture of many herbs and spices, including lemon grass, kaffir lime leaves, galangal and chillies. The ready-made paste is available from markets and supermarkets or specialty stores. It provides a convenient alternative to making your own tom yam paste.

Turmeric

This rhizome has bright-orange flesh and can be used fresh or in powder form. Be careful when handling turmeric, as it tends to stain. It was used as dye for clothing and is reputed to have antiseptic and medicinal value.

Water Chestnut

This edible dark brown tuber has crunchy cream colored flesh that is rather bland but has a slight sweetness. Choose water chestnuts with a firm texture. Water chestnuts can be eaten raw or cooked. Peel off the skin before using. If the fresh variety is unavailable, substitute with canned water chestnuts. The canned version is ready-peeled. Water chestnuts are commonly used in Asian cooking to add a pleasant crunch to stir-fried dishes, snacks and desserts. Store in the refrigerator for up to a week.

INDEX